FINGER KNITTING FUN

28 Cute, Clever, and Creative Projects for Kids

VICKIE HOWELL
Photography by Cory Ryan

Quarto is the authority on a wide range of topics.

Quarto educates, entertains and enriches the lives of our readers—enthusiasts and lovers of hands-on living.

www.QuartoKnows.com

First published in the United States of America in 2015 by
Quarry Books, an imprint of
Quarto Publishing Group USA Inc.
100 Cummings Center
Suite 406-L
Beverly, Massachusetts 01915-6101
Telephone: (978) 282-9590
Fax: (978) 283-2742
www.QuartoKnows.com
Visit our blogs at www.QuartoKnows.com

10 9 8 7 6 5 4

ISBN: 978-1-63159-070-2
Digital edition published in 2015
eISBN: 978-1-62788-324-5

Library of Congress Cataloging-in-Publication Data available

Design: Debbie Berne

Printed in China

For my three, crafty cuties

(T. D., I promise I won't tell your friends you're one of them.)

Contents

Introduction 9

1
Learn It!

How to Finger Knit 12

Two-Finger Method 14

Three-Finger Method 14

How to Join a New Color or
   Strand of Yarn 15

Fasten Off (Simple Method) 16

Fasten Off (Clean Method) 17

Finish It!

Mattress Stitch 18

Whip Stitch 19

Weaving in Ends 19

2
Wear It!

Super-Simple Neck
   Strands 23

Nice Girl Necklace 25

Rescue Wristband! 27

Cool Cuffs 29

Suede Sash 31

Fringe of Fashion 33

Bird Bangles 35

Head Turn Headband 39

Twister Scarf 41

No Sloucher Beanie 43

Daisy Chain Necklace 47

Frilly Scarf 49

3
Use It. Love It!

Vintage Bauble Blossoms 53

Tree House Garland 57

Magical Mobile 59

Tee-riffic Basket-Bag 63

Bungee Bauble 67

Snuggly Snakes 69

Little Laundry Line 71

Panda Pillow 73

Smooshy Mooshy
   Bath Mat 75

Loop-d-Loop Pillow 77

Jump Start 79

Gifter 81

Pool Key Ring 83

Planter Perfect 85

Winter's Gone Wreath 87

Tree Hugger 89

Templates 90

Suppliers 92

Acknowledgments 93

About the Author 94

Introduction

As a professional knitter (yeah, it's a thing), it's hard to remember there ever being a time when I wasn't playing with yarn. My mom had a skein in my hands as soon as I was old enough to hold it—even if it was just to wrap around things for a bit of color. Truthfully though, it wasn't until I was much older that I preferred string over stencils and knitting needles over those used for embroidery. I think I found manipulating the two sticks required for traditional hand knitting way too cumbersome for my little kid hands. So I got frustrated and moved on to other crafts.

As a mom myself now, I've experienced this passing on of craft from a different perspective. While my youngest is chomping at the bit to start knitting (she's *this* close to being ready), my older two (both teenagers now) were never that into it. Maybe when they were younger they were frustrated like I was at their age, or it could be that they didn't want to sit down long enough to learn. Who knows. It was important to me, though, that they were exposed to the possibilities that yarn holds and that they experienced it in a way that would leave a positive impression. I want all of my kiddos to see fiber as a blank canvas for creativity as well as practicality. If they have a vision; see it through. If they want to give a gift; hand make it. If they need something to keep themselves warm; produce it themselves. Whether or not they stick with it is less important—it's the awareness I was after. Enter finger knitting.

When my oldest son was about nine or so, I was writing an article on the subject for a craft website. I needed a child hand model so I asked if he'd let me teach him. Magically, he both took to it *and* liked it—it was a knitting miracle! That year for Christmas, he made scarves (much like the Twister Scarf on page 41) for all of his grandparents, parents, and stepparents. Even though his interest was brief (five years later I actually had to bribe both him and his brother to make the long pieces for Tree Hugger, page 89), it was a pretty wonderful artsy mom and son time.

This book was written with the intention of creating a ripple effect of moments like that for the kids and parents who flip through these pages. Whether it's a quick and easy project like the Snuggly Snakes (page 69), Super-Simple Neck Strands (page 23), or Jump Start Rope (page 79) that grabs fleeting attention, or the stitcher goes full, crafty throttle by making the Tee-riffic Basket Bag (page 63), Smooshy Mooshy Bath Mat (page 75), or Panda Pillow (page 73), my hope is that kids walk away knowing what it's like to put something beautiful, cool, clever, or even nonsensical into the world. Yarn is soft, but add a little creativity and it is powerful. Enjoy!

XX,

Jackie

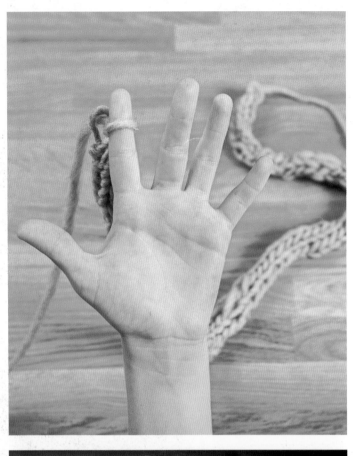

1

Learn It!

Every single project in this book begins the same way: by making at least one finger knit cord. In this section, I (with the help of some kid hands) give you step-by-step instructions on how to make these cords, providing various width options and two different ways to complete them. This is where the fun begins—enjoy!

How to Finger Knit

Traditionally, finger knitting is worked over 4 fingers (Standard Method). Sometimes, however, I like to shake things up! By working over 2 to 3 fingers, you can create a narrower piece of fabric that is a better fit for certain projects such as bracelets or belts. One thing to keep in mind is that the more fingers you use, the more even your knitted fabric will look because there's more of it to lay flat between the edge stitches. With the right materials, bumpiness can be a cool, textural design feature. Have fun and play around with it!

Standard Method

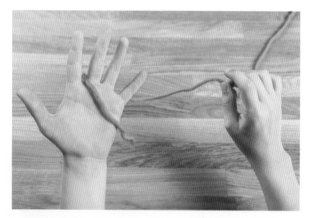

STEP 1. Leaving about a 6" (15 cm) tail, lay the yarn across the palm of your left hand (or right hand, if you're a lefty) and between the pointer finger and middle finger.

STEP 2. Using your right hand, wrap the yarn counter-clockwise around the pointer finger on your left hand.

STEP 3. Weave the yarn under and over the next 3 fingers (middle, pointer finger, and pinky); come up and around your pinky finger.

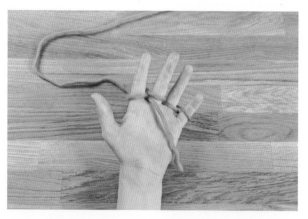

STEP 4. Weave back in the opposite direction over the next 3 fingers (ring, middle, and pointer finger). You'll now have loops on all fingers, excluding the thumb.

STEP 5. Lay the yarn across your fingers, above the loops.

STEP 6. Lift your pointer finger loop over the yarn and let it drop off your finger.

STEP 7. Continuing as in step 6, lift the loop over the yarn and let it drop off on the ring, middle, and pointer fingers. You've just completed your first row!

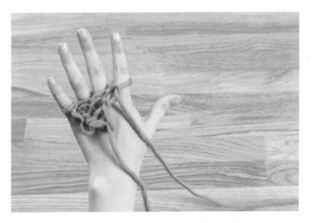

STEP 8. Repeat steps 5 through 7 until your finger-knitted cord is the desired length.

Tip Keep in mind that at the end of each row, the yarn end will be on the opposite side of the palm. Simply lay the yarn across your palm, beginning from whichever direction the yarn is oriented.

Two-Finger Method

Work the same as for Standard Method, but without wrapping yarn around your ring and pinky fingers.

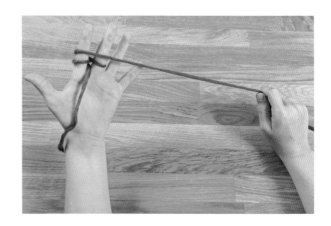

Three-Finger Method

Work the same as for Standard Method, but without wrapping yarn around your pinky.

Level Key

 These projects are super simple; you'll have them made in a snap!

 These projects might incorporate additional skills or require just a bit of parental help. You've totally got this, though!

 You're a finger knitting superstar and will go to new lengths with these projects. You'll still finger knit the same way, but will assemble your pieces to create bigger, amazing items!

How to Join a New Color or Strand of Yarn

Generally, a new color or strand of yarn should only be joined at the beginning of a row. Otherwise, you risk the possibility of a big ol' hole in your project. When you're ready, though, here's how:

STEP 1. Drop the yarn strand previously worked.

STEP 2. Leaving a tail, lay new strand across the fingers above the loops.

STEP 3. Finger knit with new strand.

STEP 4 (*Optional*) After one row is complete, tie a loose knot with the tails of the old and new strands to tighten the first stitch. Knot will be untied once you're finished with the piece and woven in with other ends.

Your Very Own Style

Don't worry if your finger-knit pieces don't look exactly like your friend's or parent's. We all have varying sizes of fingers, so our loops may be different too. Just think of the differences in weaves (open vs. tighter) as a crafty kind of fingerprint that makes you, you!

Fasten off (Simple Method)

This is the simplest way to finish off your finger knit piece—it's as easy as 1, 2, 3!

STEP 1. Cut the yarn, leaving a 6" (15 cm) tail.

STEP 2. Weave the tail through the loops, letting them fall off your fingers.

STEP 3. Pull tight and tie a knot. That's all there is to it!

General Supplies

You can pretty much finger knit with anything that can be turned into a length of string. In this book, we'll be working with everything from traditional materials like yarn and ribbon, to more alternative things like T-shirts and plastic bags. In addition to all the fun fibers we'll be knitting with, though, there are a few finishing materials that are great to have on hand. Here are just a few suggestions:

- scissors
- yarn needle
- stitch holder or pipe cleaner
- sewing needle and thread
- jewelry pliers
- hot glue sticks and glue gun

Fasten Off (Clean Method)

This method provides a more finished edge and is a great choice for projects where the ends of the pieces will be exposed. Psst . . . if you know how to knit with needles, this is just like binding off!

STEP 1. Finger knit stitches on your first two fingers.

STEP 2. Remove loop from first finger and place it on next finger. You'll now have two loops on that finger.

STEP 3. Pull bottom loop over top loop and let drop off of that finger.

STEP 4. Finger knit stitch on the next finger.
STEP 5. Repeat step 2.
STEP 6. Repeat steps 4 through 5 until one loop remains.

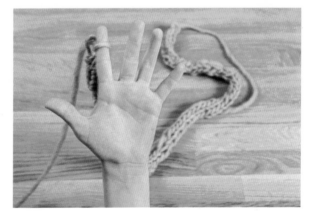

STEP 7. Cut yarn, leaving a tail. Take last loop off of your finger, feed tail through loop, and pull until snug.

Finish It!

Now that you've gotten the hang of the basics of finger knitting, here are some techniques for joining pieces together to create projects.

Mattress Stitch

This method provides a more seamless look and is great for projects that require sewing pieces together side by side. This works especially well for strips.

Watch It: Go to YouTube.com/vickiehowell for more how-to help.

STEP 1. Lay the finger-knitted pieces side by side, with the right sides facing you. If you gently pull the edge stitch away from the stitch next to it, you'll notice a row of bars between stitches.

STEP 2. Thread the yarn and needle up through the back edge of one of your pieces, inserting the needle under one of the bars, then pull the yarn through.

STEP 3. Repeat step 2, continuing to pick up bars. You'll notice your edges slowly begin to fold inward, almost hiding the seam. Continue in this manner until finished.

Whip Stitch

This is the easiest method for sewing finger-knit pieces together, and it is great for projects that require sewing finger-knit pieces into a circle or spiral.

STEP 1. With yarn and a needle, and working from back to front, come up through your piece(s).

STEP 2. Go around the piece edge(s) and repeat step 1 where you'd like to make your next stitch. The closer the repeats, the shorter the stitch length.

STEP 3. Repeat step 2 until finished, beginning the new stitch right next to the old one.

Weaving in Ends

Using a yarn needle, weave the loose ends in and out of stitches on the wrong side of work.

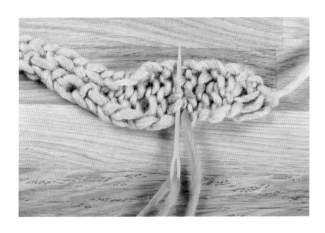

2

Wear It!

Wearable crafts are one of my favorite forms of self-expression. In this section, we'll use everything from cotton yarn to parachute cord and metallic leather to make necklaces, wristbands, scarves, a beanie, and more. You're a unique and creative kid, so pick your favorites, make them your own, and wear them with pride!

super-simple neck strands

Simple is sweet with these basic, cotton necklaces. Knit a million of these with your friends, making each unique with finishing touches!

Level

Supplies

- medium-weight cotton yarn
  (shown in Lily Sugar 'n Cream)

NOTE: Most nontoxic fabric dyes will only work on natural fibers, so cotton yarn is a must for this version!

- scissors

Finished Size

22" (56 cm)

Make It!

STEP 1. Yarn-wrap around four fingers—4 stitches.

STEP 2. Finger knit until the piece measures approximately 22" (56 cm).

STEP 3. Fasten off the end, leaving a 6" (15 cm) tail.

Finish It!

DIP-DYED VERSION

STEP 1: Mix fabric dye in cup according to manufacturer's instructions.

STEP 2: Tie one end of the necklace to a cabinet knob, while dipping about one-third of opposite end of the strand into the dye cup, placed on a counter.

STEP 3: Soak for an hour or so, and then rinse thoroughly and allow to dry.

ALL VERSIONS

STEP 4: Tie tails in a bow to form a necklace. Trim tails.

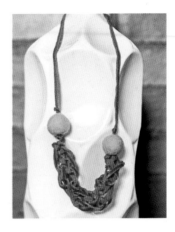

nice girl necklace

A girl can never have too many necklaces, which is a good thing. Because this velveteen beauty is so sweet, she'll want to make one to match everything in her closet!

Level

Supplies

- 2 yds (1.8 m) narrow, velveteen ribbon
- two 1" (2.5 cm) felt beads
- two jewelry O–rings
- necklace clasp
- jewelry pliers
- coordinating sewing thread and needle

Finished Size

21" (53 cm), or desired length

Make It!

STEP 1. Leaving a tail at least 8" (20.5 cm) long, yarn-wrap around four fingers—4 stitches.

STEP 2. Finger knit until the piece measures 6" (15 cm).

STEP 3. Fasten off, leaving a tail equal in length to the tail on the opposite end.

Finish It!

STEP 1. Make knots at the base of either end of the finger knitting.

STEP 2. Slide a bead onto one end of ribbon and tie another knot. Repeat for opposite end.

STEP 3. Trim ribbon to 21½" (54.5 cm), or desired length.

STEP 4. Slide an O–ring onto ribbon end, fold ribbon over ¼" (6 mm) and hand sew down.

STEP 5. For opposite end, slide an O–ring onto end and add jewelry clasp. Then repeat finishing instructions in step 4.

NOTE. For a simpler route, skip the O–rings and tie the ends to form necklace.

Hey, Parents!

This makes a great party craft! Set up a table with various colors of ribbons, beads, and findings and let the necklace making begin!

rescue wristband!

Backyards can be perilous, so you never know when you're going to need some paracord. Wear it as a wristband, and then you'll always be prepared for that next outdoor adventure!

Level

Supplies

- package parachute cord
- set plastic parachute cord clasps
- lighter or hot glue sticks and glue gun (**ADULT SUPERVISION REQUIRED!**)

Finished Size

7" (18 cm) long or desired length

Make It!

STEP 1. Yarn-wrap the cord around 2 fingers only (pointer and middle)—2 stitches.

STEP 2. Finger knit until piece measures 8" (20.5 cm), or 1" (2.5 cm) longer than wrist measurement.

STEP 3. Fasten off.

Finish It!

STEP 1. Attach the buckles to either end of piece by tying on, and then trim.

STEP 2. Ask an adult to use a lighter to melt cord ends securely to the bracelet. Alternatively, the ends could be hot glued down.

cool cuffs

Leather lacing isn't just for moccasins! Metallic versions of the material will give a modern feel to these bad-a*@ bracelets!

Level

Supplies

- 3 yds (2.7 m) leather lacing
- O−ring and jewelry clasp set (optional)
- hot glue sticks and glue gun

Finished Size

5½" (14 cm) long, or desired length

Make It!

STEP 1. Yarn-wrap around three fingers—3 stitches.

STEP 2. Finger knit until the piece measures 4½" (11.5 cm) or 1" (2.5 cm) shorter than the wrist.

STEP 3. Fasten off.

Finish It!

STEP 1. Tie ends to form bracelet or attach an O−ring and jewelry clasp as follows: Slide O−ring onto one end of piece, fold over about ½" (1.3 cm) from the base of finger knitting to form a loop, wrap lacing around the knot a couple of times.

STEP 2. Trim lacing and secure the tail with hot glue.

STEP 3. Repeat process with jewelry clasp on opposite end.

suede sash

A belt can keep your britches up or just make your outfit extra awesome.
This moccasin-inspired sash uses suede lacing and beads to create a Boho-chic
accessory that will add a dash of style to any wardrobe.

Level

Supplies

- 10 yds (9 m) suede lacing
- 2 to 4 large-holed beads

Finished Size

46" (117 cm) or desired length,
excluding beads and tails

Make It!

STEP 1. Yarn-wrap the lacing around two fingers—
2 stitches.

STEP 2. Finger knit until piece measures 46" (117 cm).

STEP 3. Fasten off, leaving 6" (15 cm) tail.

Finish It!

STEP 1. Tie knots at the base of the finger knitting.

STEP 2. Slide bead(s) onto the tail; tie a knot.

STEP 3. Repeat step 2 for opposite end.

Tip Using a stiffer material such as suede and knitting only two stitches will give you a bumpier piece. If texture isn't your thing, consider using a smoother, more pliable material like nylon cording or yarn and working with 3 to 4 stitches instead!

fringe of fashion

A plain, finger-knit strand is transformed into an on-trend necklace by simply adding some neon and neutral flair. Go fashion forward with some fringe!

Level

Supplies

- neon yarn (shown in Caron Simply Soft, neon yellow)
- neutral yarn (shown in Patons Glam Stripe, silver)

Finished Size

22" (56 cm)

Make It!

Work the same way as for Super-Simple Neck Strands, page 23.

Finish It!

STEP 1. Holding the neon and neutral yarns together, cut eight (four of each color), 6" (15 cm) strands.

STEP 2. Holding strands together, fold in half to create loop for next step.

STEP 3. Fold loop over the necklace strand, and pull the ends of yarn through the loop. Pull tight. First fringe bit is now complete.

STEP 4. Repeat steps 2 and 3 four more times, creating a total of five fringe bits.

STEP 5. Trim if necessary to make even.

STEP 6. Tie the tails in a bow to form a necklace. Trim tails.

Tip Are you feeling fancy? Opt for adding metal jewelry clasps (see Nice Girl Necklace, page 25) instead of tying the tails to close the strand!

bird bangles

Turn string into fabric with the magic of handfelting. You'll be amazed how
a little elbow grease and some beads can make beautiful bangles!

Level

Supplies

- bulky, 100% wool yarn (shown in Patons Classic
  Roving, Natural; Low Tide; Frosted Plum)

- yarn needle

- mild soap or shampoo

- sink or bowl with hot water

- coordinating sewing thread and needle

- beads or buttons

Finished Size

Size shown here fits over a 6" (15 cm) hand.

Make It!

STEP 1. Yarn-wrap around 4 fingers—4 stitches.

STEP 2. Finger knit until the piece measures 8"
(20.5 cm), or approximately 30 percent longer than
the wrist measurement.

STEP 3. Fasten off.

Five More Great Ways to Embellish Your Bangles

1. Wrap contrasting cording or string over a
   portion of bangle and tack down.

2. Cross-stitch a design on it.

3. Embroider your name on it.

4. Sew on a few small, artificial flowers
   around it.

5. Hot glue on some metal studs or
   plastic gems.

Finish It!

Thread the tail onto yarn needle, sew ends together to make circle, and weave in the ends.

HAND FELT

STEP 1. Fill a bowl or sink with hottish water (making it no warmer than your hands can handle) and 1 tablespoon (15 ml) of mild soap.

STEP 2. Vigorously scrunch and rub the wool against itself—agitation is key when felting, so have at it!

STEP 3. After a couple of minutes, stop to check your work. If the piece has shrunk and you can no longer see the stitch definition, then you're done. If not, keep going.

STEP 4. Rinse the piece with cool water, squeezing out the excess.

STEP 5. Shape into a bracelet and allow it to dry.

EMBELLISH

Sew on beads or buttons.

NOTE. Felting only works with yarns made of 100 percent animal fibers, so be sure to check the label for fiber content before you get started!

Classroom Idea

Hey, teachers! Even though felting isn't an exact science, the general rule is that your knit piece will shrink approximately 30 percent when felted. This number can vary, however, based on the thickness of the yarn and openness of the stitches. Experiment in the classroom with lengths finger knit by knitters with different-size hands (i.e. adults and kids) and using varying weights of yarn. Do the math and record the results for a great lesson on percentages!

head turn headband

Turn a plain band on its head with this simple, spiral embellishment. You and your friends will have a blast customizing versions for every day of the week! Change up the colors *and* the materials to make each accessory unique!

Level

Supplies

- scraps, bulky, multicolored yarn (shown in Patons ColorWul, Bramble)
- headband
- yarn needle
- decorative buttons
- hot glue sticks and glue gun

Finished Size

3" (7.5 cm)

Make It!

STEP 1. Yarn-wrap around four—4 stitches.

STEP 2. Finger knit until the piece measures 12" (30.5 cm).

STEP 3. Fasten off.

Finish It!

STEP 1. Weave in the ends.

STEP 2. Roll piece into a spiral, and glue to headband.

STEP 3. Glue the buttons to the center of spiral.

twister scarf

This project puts a new twist on finger-knit strands, so step up your skills by braiding a colorful scarf!

Level

Supplies

- 3 different colors/textures of similar weight yarn (shown in Bernat Softee Chunky, Glowing Gold; Bernat Soft Boucle, Natural; and Patons ColorWul, Countryside)
- yarn needle
- tape

Finished Size

Approximately 45" (114.5 cm)

Hey, Kids!

Make these for your parents and grandparents for the holidays. They'll love 'em!

Make It!

(Make 3; one in each yarn type.)

STEP 1. Yarn-wrap around four fingers—4 stitches.

STEP 2. Finger knit until the piece measures approximately 48" (122 cm)

STEP 3. Fasten off.

Finish It!

STEP 1. Tape the ends of all 3 pieces to a table or floor.

STEP 2. Braid pieces together.

STEP 3. Using a yarn needle and a strand of yarn, tack pieces together by sewing an X at either end of the braid.

STEP 4. Weave in ends.

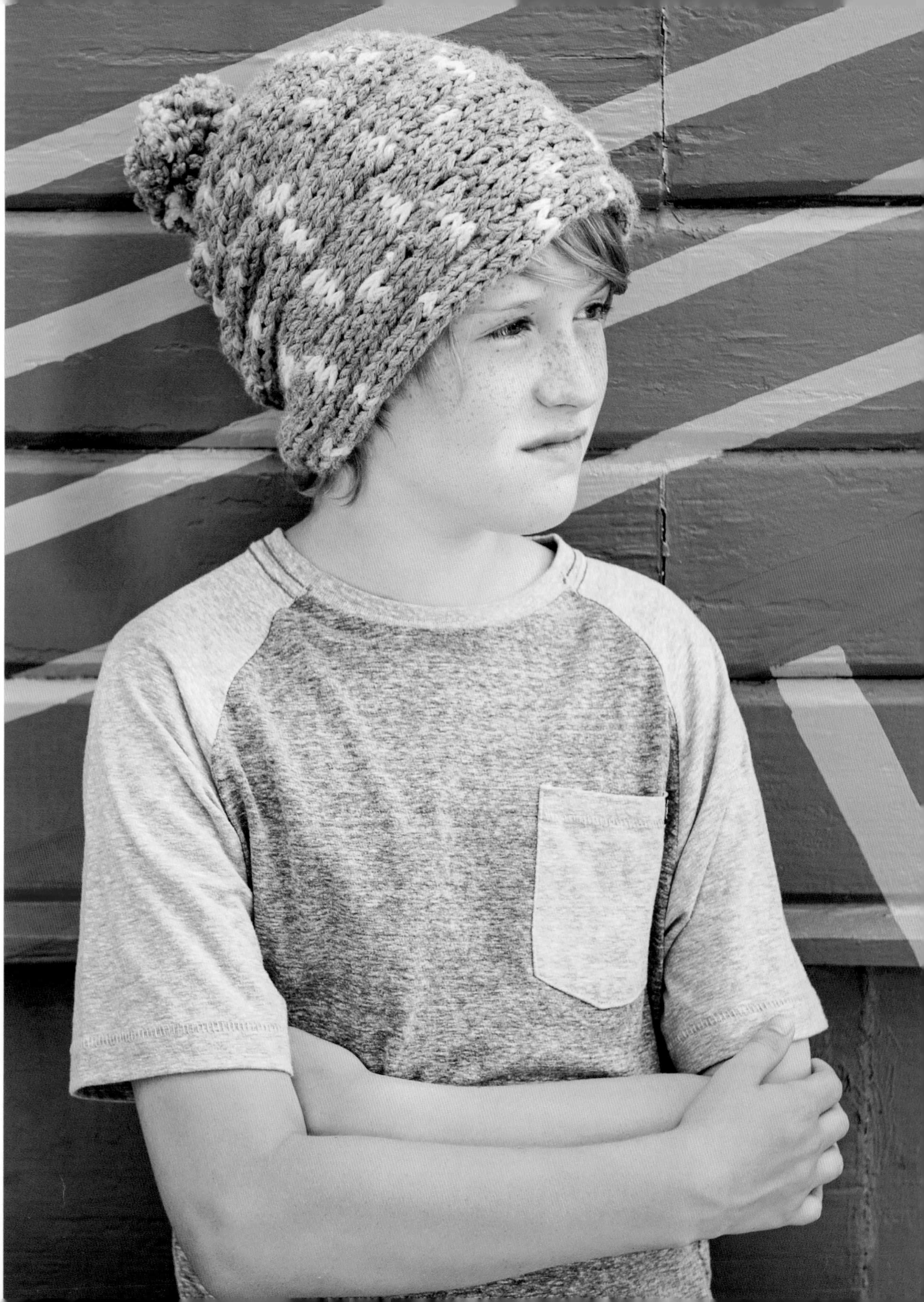

no sloucher beanie

Every hip kid needs a cool hat, and this slouchy beanie fills the bill!

Level

Supplies

- 4 oz. (115 g) chunky-weight yarn, in grey and neon
- tapestry needle
- 3" (7.6 cm) piece of cardboard

Finished Size

Fits up to 20" (51 cm) head

Make It!

STEP 1. Yarn-wrap around four fingers—4 stitches.

STEP 2. Finger knit for about 13½' (4 m)

STEP 3. Fasten off, leaving a generous tail.

Finish It!

ASSEMBLE BEANIE

STEP 1. Make a 20" (51 cm) circle with the end of piece; use a tapestry needle and yarn to sew into place. You now have a hat brim.

STEP 2. Wrap the piece in spiraling formation, taking care to measure every round to ensure circumference stays the same, using mattress stitch to sew rounds together until the tube measures 11" (28 cm) from brim edge. If you have extra finger knitting left, unravel and refasten off. If you come up short, use the tail to finger knit the needed amount.

STEP 3. Fasten off, leaving at a generous tail.

CLOSE BEANIE

STEP 1. Thread a tapestry needle with yarn tail and stitch top-center points of front and back together; pinch the side edges to the same center point and stitch. The top of the hat will now be in a star formation.

STEP 2. Continue to pinch the opposite edges and stitch them together until top of the hat is completely closed.

STEP 3. Fasten off; feed the tail through top of hat to the inside.

MAKE THE POM-POM

STEP 1. Using a 3" (7.5 cm) piece of cardboard, wrap the yarn around cardboard about 50 times.

STEP 2. Slip wraps off cardboard and tie a piece of yarn tightly around the center of the wraps, leaving a tail.

STEP 3. Cut both ends of wraps and fluff pom-pom. Trim to even it out.

STEP 4. Thread tail through tapestry needle and sew pom-pom to top of beanie.

STEP 5. Weave in ends.

Tip Need to take a break before finishing your project? No problem! A pipe cleaner makes a great stitch holder! Simply feed it through the live loops on your fingers, slip loops off your fingers, bend the pipe cleaner, and twist ends to form a ring. When you're ready, just slip the loops back onto your fingers and go!

daisy chain necklace

Braids and chains make a happy necklace bed for a loopy, flower adornment. Save this project for a backyard craft date. After all, what better way to spend a summer's day with your fellow, jewelry-loving friends?

Level

Supplies

- 2 colors, medium-weight yarn (shown in Bernat Sheep[ish] by Vickie Howell, [A] Chartreuse[ish] and [B] Olive[ish])
- 1" (2.5 cm) button
- yarn needle and thread or hot glue sticks and glue gun

Finished Size

24" (61 cm)

Make It!

KNIT STRANDS

STEP 1. With color A, yarn-wrap around your four fingers—4 stitches.

STEP 2. Finger knit until the piece measures 22" (56 cm).

STEP 3. Fasten off.

STEP 4. Repeat steps 1 through 3 with color B.

BRAIDS

STEP 1. Using 3 strands of the same color yarn for each braid, make one 22" (56 cm) braid in color B and one 24" (61 cm) braid in color A.

Finish It!

Excluding the knit piece in color B, hold all strands and sew or tie ends together to form a necklace.

MAKE FLOWER

STEP 1. Fold color B knit strand to create petal loops, using a yarn needle to tack petals in place.

STEP 2. Sew a flower on joined area of necklace. Trim the ends to create fringe.

STEP 3. Sew or hot glue a button to flower center.

frilly scarf

No frills are for fools with this gloriously girly scarf—embrace the ruffles and rule the world!

Level

Supplies

- 1 ball ruffle yarn (shown in Patons Pirouette, Midnight Blue Shimmer)
- yarn needle

Finished Size

48" (122 cm) long

Make It!

STEP 1. Leaving a tail for weaving in, place a loop (which exists within the ruffle yarn) on each of your four fingers—4 stitches.

STEP 2. Lay ruffle yarn across fingers, placing an addition loop on each finger; lift the bottom pinky loop over top loop and let drop off the finger; continue in that manner for the remaining fingers. The first row is now complete!

STEP 3. Repeat finger knitting as established (watching ruffles form as you go) until the scarf measures 48" (122 cm).

STEP 4. Fasten off.

Finish It!

Weave in ends.

3

Use It. Love It!

Are you looking to make something
useful? You'll find projects made for
cuddling, playing, decorating, or toting
your favorite things in this section. From
a tree house garland to a panda pillow
and a tote bag made entirely of repurposed
T-shirts, these pages will inspire you to
create unexpected novelties while having a
whole lotta finger knitting fun!

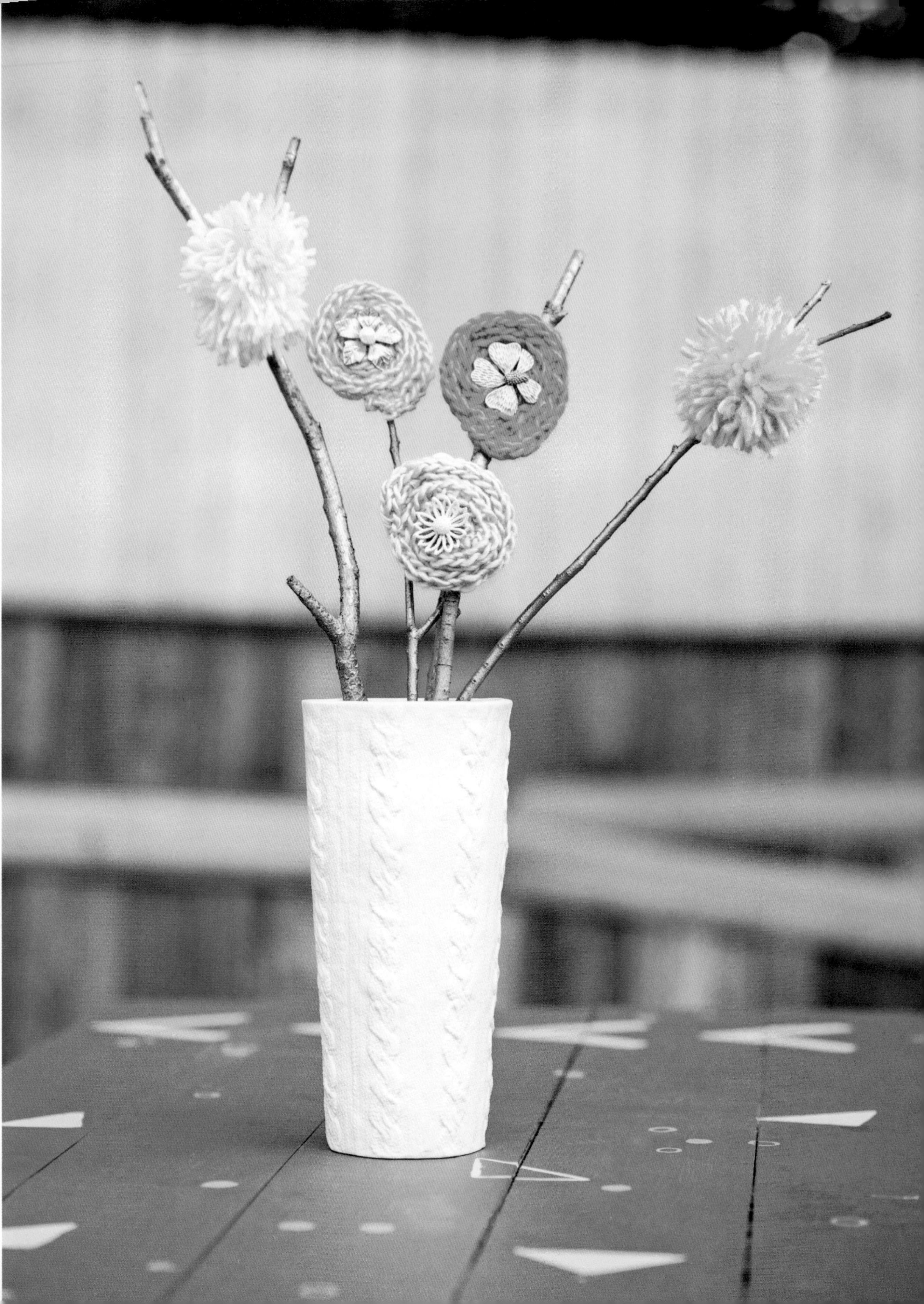

vintage bauble blossoms

A little yarn and some flower pins scored from a thrift store create some pretty petals. Throw in branches from the yard and a touch of paint and you'll have a bouquet of bright and beautiful blossoms!

Level

Supplies

- medium-weight yarn in 5 colors (shown in Bernat Sheep(ish) by Vickie Howell, Chartreuse(ish), Hot Pink(ish), Robin's Egg(ish), Yellow(ish), and White(ish))
- yarn needle
- small tree branches
- vintage flower brooches or earrings
- hot glue sticks and glue gun
- gold spray paint, optional
- 3" (7.5 cm) piece of cardboard

Finished Size

The blossoms are approximately 3 ½" (9 cm) circles.

Make It!

(Make 3; one in each color.)

STEP 1. Yarn wrap around four fingers—4 stitches.

STEP 2. Finger knit until the piece measures approximately 22" (56 cm).

STEP 3. Fasten off, leaving long tail for sewing.

Finish It!

CREATE BLOSSOMS

STEP 1. Roll the piece into a spiral blossom.

STEP 2. Thread the tail into yarn needle and whip stitch piece together. Weave in the ends.

STEP 3. Repeat steps 1 and 2 to create each blossom.

POM-POMS

(Make 1 of each, in the remaining 2 colors.)

STEP 1. Using a 3" (7.5 cm) piece of cardboard, wrap the yarn around cardboard approximately 50 times. Slip wraps off cardboard and tie a piece of yarn tightly around the center of the wraps, leaving a tail.

STEP 2. Cut both ends of the wraps and fluff the pom-pom. Trim, but not too perfectly—a little scraggly looks cute!

PAINT BRANCHES (OPTIONAL)

Spray paint the branches. Let dry.

ASSEMBLE

STEP 1. Hot glue vintage baubles to blossom centers.

STEP 2. Glue a blossom or pom-pom to each branch.

Spiral Bound

Are you not feeling the flower power? No biggie—these spiral motifs are bound for other things! Here are a few more ideas:

1. Ditch the vintage pins and simply sew plain versions on a pillow for some polka-dot patterning.

2. Make them a bit larger and in jute or cord for some cool coasters.

3. Sew two together and stuff with poly-fil fiber for some dollhouse floor cushions.

tree house garland

Any fort is made more festive with decorations, so add some pep to your playhouse with this pop-y garland!

Level

Supplies

- skein medium-weight yarn (shown in Caron United, Grey Heather)
- 12 plastic bulb ornaments

Finished Size

96" (244 cm) long

Make It!

STEP 1. Prestring the bulbs onto yarn.

STEP 2. Yarn-wrap around four fingers—4 stitches.

STEP 3. Finger knit for approximately 8" (20.5 cm).

STEP 4. Add the bulb to the piece by knitting first 2 stitches, pushing bulb up to palm, and knit last 2 stitches. On next row, knit to the bulb, slip worked loops from fingers, push the bulb so it hangs downward (away from back of hand), place the loops back on your fingers, continue knitting to end.

STEP 5. Repeat steps 3 and 4 eleven more times (or until all bulbs are placed).

STEP 6. Finger knit approximately 8" (20.5 cm) more.

STEP 7. Fasten off.

Finish It!

Tie loops with the yarn tails at each end, and hang your garland where desired.

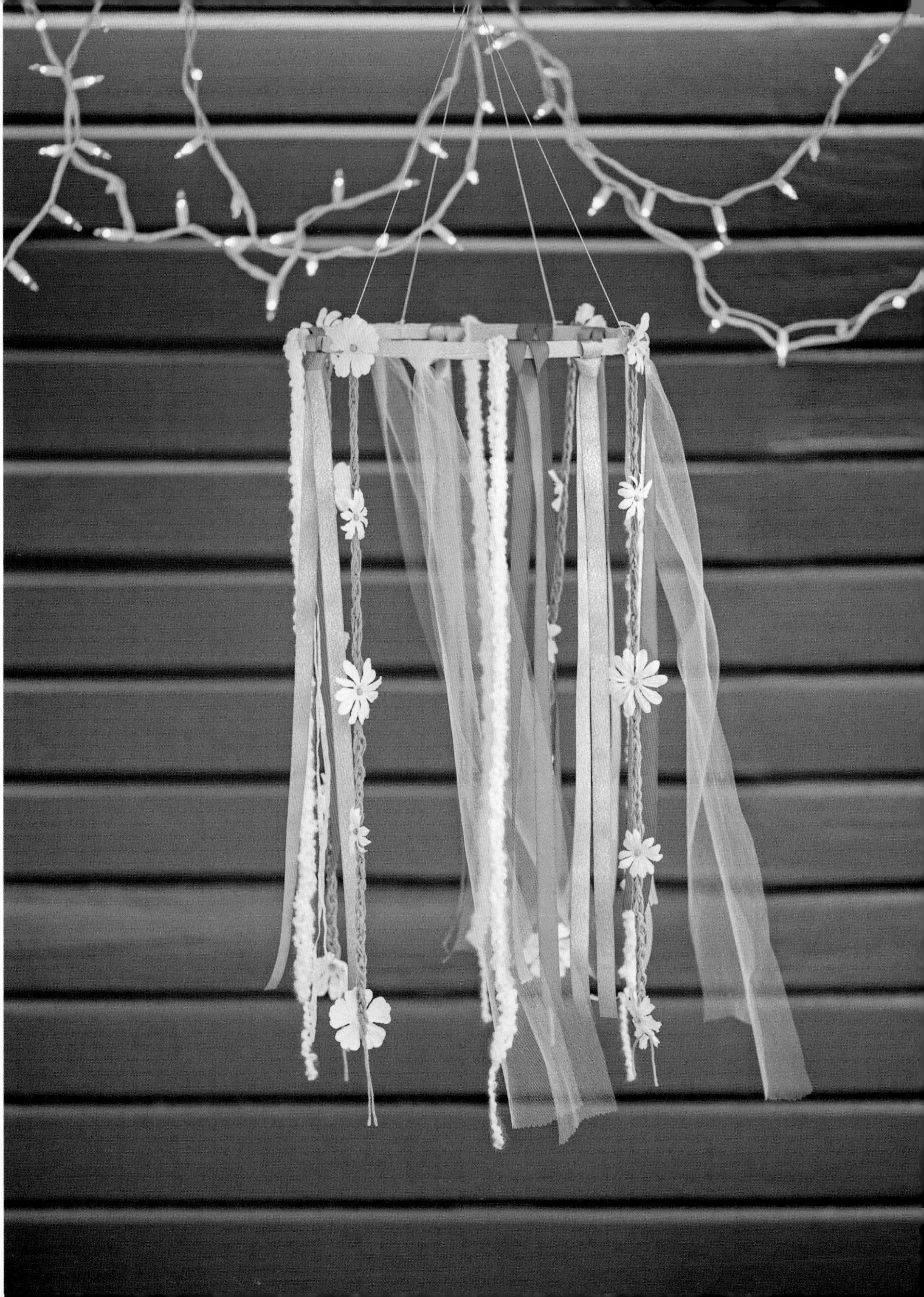

magical mobile

Add a little dreaminess to your room with a beribboned mobile. Simple strands of different materials create a lovely decoration that's both whimsical and Boho chic. Make it and enjoy the magic!

Level

Supplies

- sport-weight yarn (shown in Bernat Cotton[ish] by Vickie Howell, Turquoise Terry Cloth)
- worsted-weight, textured yarn (shown in Bernat Soft Boucle, Natural)
- 5–6 yds (4.6–5.5 m) each, of four different colors of ribbon and tulle
- 2 yds (1.8 m) string
- 12" (30.5 cm) embroidery hoop (nonhardware half only)
- washi tape
- 20 paper flowers
- hot glue sticks and glue gun

Finished Size

The mobile hangs approximately 36" (91.5 cm) depending on length of hanging strings.

Make It!

PREP EMBROIDERY HOOP

Wrap washi tape around the hoop until completely covered. Set aside.

FINGER KNIT STRANDS
(Make 4 in each of two yarns.)

NOTE. For sport-weight yarn, consider using two strands held together as one.

STEP 1. Yarn-wrap around four fingers—4 stitches.

STEP 2. Finger knit until the piece measures approximately 26" (66 cm).

STEP 3. Fasten off. Trim tails to approximately 2" (5 cm).

Finish It!

STEP 1. Glue 5 flowers onto each sport-weight yarn strand and textured strand.

STEP 2. Evenly space and glue the strands onto the embroidery hoop.

STEP 3. Cut the ribbon and tulle into 48" (122 cm) lengths. Attach each length to hoop where desired, using a slip knot as follows: fold ribbon in half, then fold it over the hoop to create a loop; feed the tails through the loop and pull to secure.

STEP 4. Cut the string into 4 even lengths. Evenly disperse and tie the pieces to the hoop. Knot all 4 strands together approximately 3" (7.5 cm) from top, then again 1" (2.5 cm) from the top to create a hanging loop.

Tip Make your finger-knitting strands longer to transform them into a bed curtain.

Fun Fact!

Before the current Guinness World Record was held by a German man, an 11-year-old New Zealand girl, named Gemma Pouls, set the finger knitting record with a 2.78 kilometer (approximately 3,040 yard) strand!

tee-riffic basket-bag

Giving ratty ol' T-shirts a new life is in the bag with this upcycled carry-all!

Level

Supplies

- 8 to 10 Men's L/XL T-shirts
- fabric scissors
- yarn needle
- safety pin

Finished Size

Approximately 14" (35.5 cm) across at base

Make It!

CREATE T-SHIRT YARN

(See the sidebar, "Making T-Shirt Yarn.")

STEP 1. Yarn-wrap over four fingers—4 stitches.

STEP 2. Finger knit piece until piece measures approximately 4½' (14 m), tying on new T-shirt yarn ends as you run out.

STEP 3. Fasten off.

Making T-Shirt Yarn

1. Gather T-shirts to be recycled (the bigger the shirt, the better).

2. Cut off the sleeves and lay T-shirts flat, horizontally.

3. Using a rotary cutter (recommended) or scissors, cut T-shirts into 1" (2.5 cm) strips (they don't need to be perfect). Snip each piece on the side seam, so that it's one long strip instead of a circle.

4. Stretch the strip out so that the edges curl in.

5. Tie strips together using a square knot and roll into a ball.

Finish It!

ASSEMBLE BAG BOTTOM

STEP 1. Beginning at what will be the center of the bag base, begin spiraling the piece to create a flat circle (think cinnamon roll).

STEP 2. Using a strand of T-shirt yarn and a needle, whip stitch the layered rounds together until the circle measures 14" (35.5 cm) across. Place safety pin at this point to mark the end of round.

ASSEMBLE BAG SIDES

STEP 1. Continue spiraling and sewing as established, but begin stacking the rounds so they no longer lay flat to build the sides of the bag. Stop spiraling when the sides measure approximately 13" (33 cm) from the base of the bag (or until you have enough length left for 1 round, plus 8" [20.5 cm]).

HANDLE ROUND

STEP 1. Lay the bag flat on a table so it rests on the front or back and *continue sewing in a spiral until 2½" (6.5 cm) from the center point of the top edge of the front. Measure 8" (20.5 cm) of finger knit piece, whip stitch around bag body only (not attaching handle portion) for 5" (12.5 cm); resume sewing in a spiral around front edge and around to "back." Repeat from * one more time; finish sewing the round.

STEP 2. Sew down end, secure with a knot, and trim.

NOTE. If you have extra length, just unravel the excess and fasten off before sewing down.

STEP 3. Weave in or trim ends.

Recycle!

You can use cut-up plastic grocery bags for this project, too!

Make it Work!

Want to change the size of the basket-bag, but not sure how long to make your strand? Simply sew as you go! Knit a length and without fastening off your working end's yarn, begin the assembly process. Once you get the majority sewn, start knitting again. Repeat until you're finished!

bungee bauble

Loop this decorative lanyard out of bungee cord and say goodbye
to a boring ol' backpack!

Level

Supplies

- package bungee cord
- 1½" (4 cm) lanyard clip
- charm on an O–ring (optional)
- hot glue sticks and glue gun

Finished Size

Approximately 7" (18 cm), excluding
clasp and charm

Make It!

STEP 1. Leaving a 6" (15 cm) tail, yarn-wrap the cord
around three fingers—3 stitches.

STEP 2. Finger knit until the piece measures
approximately 6" (15 cm).

STEP 3. Fasten off.

Finish It!

STEP 1. Slide the clip onto the tail, fold tail over to
make ½" (1 cm) loop, knot into place, and trim.

STEP 2. Make several knots on the opposite end of the
tail or tie a charm into place and trim.

STEP 3. With an adult's supervision, hot glue the
trimmed ends to the lanyard to secure.

Psst! This project would make a
great Father's Day gift!

snuggly snakes

A softie snake that's easy to make will put a smile on any reptile lover's face!

Level

Supplies

- bulky yarn scraps
- set of colorful googly eyes
- yarn needle
- hot glue gun or fabric glue
- felt scraps

Finished Size

18" (45.5 cm) long

Make It!

STEP 1. Yarn-wrap around four fingers—4 stitches.

STEP 2. Finger knit until the piece measures 18" (45.5 cm).

STEP 3. Fasten off.

STEP 4. Using a needle and yarn, sew a stitch on the underside of where you want your snake's head to end to cinch it.

Finish It!

STEP 1. Weave in ends.

STEP 2. Cut tongue template from felt scrap.

STEP 3. Glue on eyes and tongue.

Tongue template

Copy at 100%.

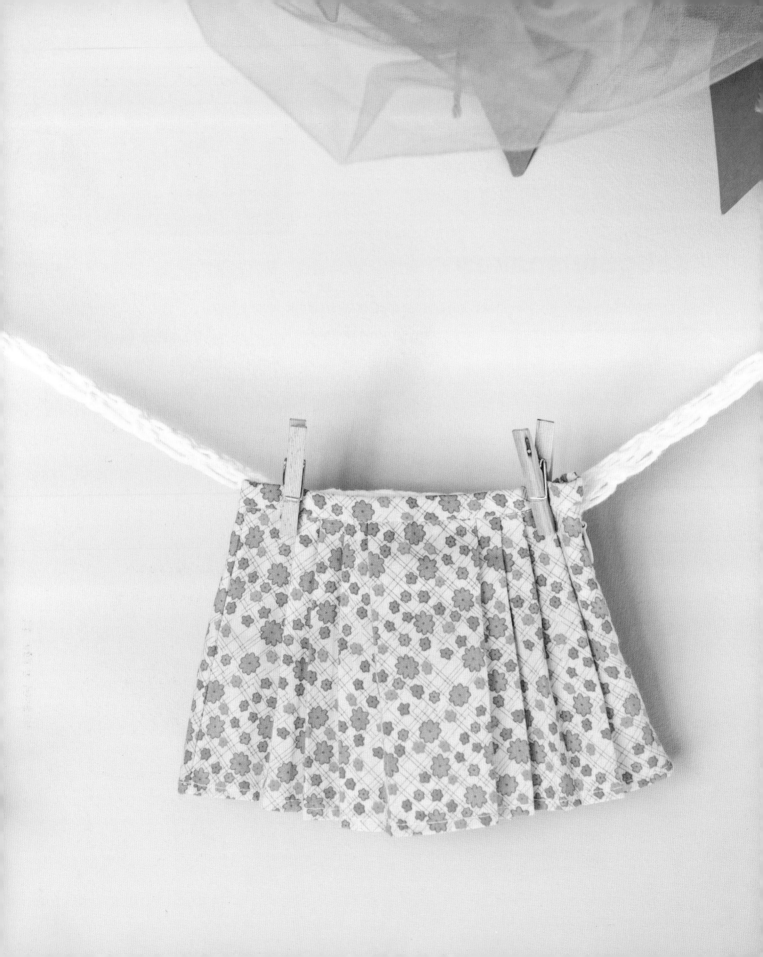

little laundry line

Dirty laundry won't be a worry for Dolly, when her wee wardrobe is on this clothesline.

Level

Supplies

- medium-weight, cotton yarn (shown in Lily Sugar 'n Cream, White)
- mini clothespins

Finished Size

24" (61 cm) long

Make It!

STEP 1. Yarn-wrap around four fingers—4 stitches.

STEP 2. Finger knit until the piece measures 24" (61 cm).

STEP 3. Fasten off.

Finish It!

STEP 1. Tie knots at each end of the clothesline.

STEP 2. Tie the tail ends in slip knots for hanging

Five Things to Make with One Strand

1. Ponytail tie

2. Friendship bracelet

3. Holiday tree garland

4. Play action figure zip-line

5. Shoelace

panda pillow

This cute little cushion makes for a perfect panda pal!

Level

Finished Size

9" (23 cm) square

Supplies

- ball chunky-weight yarn in white (shown in Patons Wool Roving, Aran)
- medium-weight yarn scraps, white
- sheet black felt
- white felt scraps
- fabric glue
- black sewing thread and needle
- sewing pins
- yarn needle
- measuring tape
- 9" x 9" (23 x 23 cm) pillow form
- templates (page 90–91)

Make It!

STEP 1. Yarn-wrap around four fingers—4 stitches.

STEP 2. Finger knit piece until it measures approximately 16½' (5 m) from end.

STEP 3. Fasten off.

ASSEMBLE PILLOW BODY

STEP 1. Fold the first 8" (20.5 cm) of the piece over and use a yarn needle and medium-weight yarn to stitch end in place, forming a ring. This forms the base of your 9" (23 cm) pillow cover.

STEP 2. Using the bottom ring as a guide, wrap piece in spiral rounds, whipstitching to the round below as you go—until pillow cover measures 9" (23 cm) across (when laid flat.) Stitch end in place, then stitch across open top to close. Insert pillow form; sew closed.

Finish It!

STEP 1. Scan and print templates for face and ears (page 90). Using templates as a guide, cut out felt pieces.

STEP 2. Pinch the ears to create a pleated effect, pin in place, and hand sew using a needle and thread.

STEP 3. Sew or glue face pieces to pillow front.

smooshy mooshy bath mat

Whether you place it near the bath or in your bedroom, you'll step sweetly onto this cute and comfy mat.

Level

Supplies

- 14 oz. (400 g) bulky fleece yarn (shown in Bernat Baby Blanket, [A] Little Petunias, [B] Vanilla)
- tapestry needle

Finished Size

Approximately 27" x 18" (69 cm x 46 cm)

Make It!

FINGER KNIT PIECES

(Make 12 in color A, and 9 in color B.)
STEP 1. Yarn-wrap around four fingers—4 stitches.

STEP 2. Finger knit until the piece measures 36" (91.5 cm).

STEP 3. Fasten off.

BRAIDS

STEP 1. With color A, braid 3 strands together.

STEP 2. Using a tapestry needle and yarn, tack either end of braid to keep the pieces in place.

STEP 3. Repeat steps 1 and 2 three times more to make a total of 4 braids.

STEP 4. Repeat steps 1 and 2 with color B, three times, making 3 braids.

Finish It!

STEP 1. Arrange the braids side by side on a table or floor, alternating braids made with color A with those made using color B to create a striped bath mat.

STEP 2. Sew the tips of each braid together.

STEP 3. Work your way down the braids, sewing them together every few inches until all are secure.

STEP 4. Weave in ends.

loop-d-loop pillow

Has store-bought room decor got you down? No problem. Any drab pillow can become your canvas for creativity. Simply add a pop of finger-knit color to "draw" a design!

Level

Supplies

- medium-weight yarn (shown in Bernat Sheep[ish] by Vickie Howell, Turquoise[ish])
- sewing needle and thread
- sewing pins
- 20" x 16" (51 x 41 cm) pillow

Make It!

STEP 1. Yarn-wrap around four fingers—4 stitches.

STEP 2. Finger knit until the piece measures approximately 65" (165 cm).

STEP 3. Fasten off.

Finish It!

STEP 1. Weave in ends.

STEP 2. Lay the piece on a pillow in a loop-d-loop pattern, pin in place, and tack down in several areas with a sewing needle and thread.

Tip Use this same method to embellish a friend's name on a pillow or tote bag with a strand of finger knitting!

jump start

Jump ropes are a great, first-time finger-knitting project. They're easy to create and fun to use, so gather your friends to take the finger-knitting leap—make this classic favorite for your next school field day!

Level

Supplies

- ball chunky-weight cotton yarn
- set of jump rope handles
- yarn needle

Finished Size

70" (178 cm) or desired length

Make It!

STEP 1. Yarn-wrap around three fingers—3 stitches.

STEP 2. Finger knit until the piece measures approximately 5¾' (3.4 m).

STEP 3. Fasten off.

Finish It!

Using a tail end as a lead, pull through the jump rope handle hole, knot firmly into place, and trim the tail. Repeat for opposite end.

Thrift Tip! Harvest some handles on the cheap. Check your local second-hand store for an old jump rope to deconstruct.

gifter

Sometimes how pretty a package is on the outside can be as smile-inducing as the contents on the inside. Add some finger-knit flair to any gift with this one-of-a-kind bow!

Level

Supplies

- medium-weight yarn (shown in Bernat Sheep[ish] by Vickie Howell, Robin's Egg(ish))

Make It!

STEP 1. Yarn-wrap around four fingers—4 stitches.

STEP 2. Finger knit until the piece measures approximately 30" (76 cm).

STEP 3. Fasten off.

Finished Size

Approximately 4" (11.5 cm)

Finish It!

STEP 1. With the wrong side facing up, layer the piece on top of itself as if it were taffy, creating a series of stacked loops. See diagram below, left.

STEP 2. Pinch the center of the stacked loops and wrap a piece of yarn around the center several times, tying a knot underneath to secure (be sure to leave very long tails for attaching the bow to the package).

STEP 3. Gently separate the loops to give the look of a flower bloom, exposing the wrong side of the knitted piece to show fabric bumps.

STEP 4. Attach it to a gift by tying or taping it in place.

Tip Try making bows with a variety of materials to create different looks. Thin ribbon, raffia, or silk cord would all work beautifully!

pool key ring

You'll unlock the secrets of summer fun when you make this ring for
the pool gate's key!

Level

Supplies

- package plastic lacing
- yarn needle
- charm
- key ring

Finished Size

3" (7.5 cm)

Make It!

STEP 1. Yarn-wrap the lacing around four fingers—
4 stitches.

STEP 2. Finger knit until piece measures 7" (9.5 cm).

STEP 3. Fasten off, leaving a 6" (15 cm) tail.

Finish It!

STEP 1. Thread tail through yarn needle and sew
together the end and beginning of the piece to form
ring.

STEP 2. Slide the charm and key ring onto the tail, fold
the tail over and wrap it around the base a couple of
times, then tie a knot.

STEP 3. Weave in the end and trim.

planter perfect

Let your imagination bloom while you decorate a simple terra-cotta pot. Each little added detail will surely plant the seeds for your very own creatively cool garden!

Level

Supplies

- ball chunky, jute rope
- terra-cotta pot, any size
- gold-leaf paint
- paintbrush
- decorative ribbon, long enough to fit the circumference of the pot top
- hot-glue sticks and glue gun
- large-eye yarn needle

Make It!

STEP 1. Yarn-wrap around three fingers—3 stitches.

STEP 2. Finger knit until the piece measures long enough to fit around the circumference of the pot's widest point, which is just below the lip.

STEP 3. Fasten off and set aside.

STEP 4. Paint the lip of the pot. Let dry.

Finish It!

STEP 1. Weave in ends.

STEP 2. Use hot glue to secure the cozy to the pot.

STEP 3. Glue the ribbon to the pot lip.

winter's gone wreath

Wave bye-bye to winter's cold by making this happy wreath and hanging it in your home! Or, choose holiday colors and themed fabric to tailor it to any celebration throughout the year.

Level

Supplies

- ball furry yarn (shown in Bernat Pipsqueak, Lime)
- 12" (30.5 cm) foam wreath (or desired size)
- yarn needle
- scraps of felt and fabric in various colors
- 5 button covers (1 large, 4 medium)
- hot-glue sticks and glue gun
- 9" (23 cm) length of ribbon

Finished Size

12" (30.5 cm)

Make It!

STEP 1. Yarn-wrap around four fingers—4 stitches.

STEP 2. Finger knit until the piece is long enough to completely the cover wreath—this will vary based on the yarn.

STEP 3. Fasten off.

Finish It!

STEP 1. Weave in the beginning tail end.

STEP 2. Starting anywhere on the back of the wreath, secure end of the piece to foam using hot glue.

STEP 3. Wrap yarn around the wreath several times and glue down to secure. Repeat this process until the wreath is completely covered.

STEP 4. Fasten off (if you haven't already). Weave in the remaining end and glue it down.

STEP 5. Follow the manufacturer's instructions to cover the button covers with fabric.

STEP 6. Measure and cut felt circles that are approximately ½" (1 cm) larger than the buttons, and snip edges all the way around to create petals.

STEP 7. Glue the felt and buttons off-center on the bottom of the wreath.

STEP 8. Fold the ribbon into a loop and glue the ends to the top-back of the wreath.

tree hugger

Take your first steps into the world of public art by creating this colorful cozy for a tree trunk using a little yarn graffiti (a.k.a. yarn bombing!). Grab some friends and decorate a tree or two in your favorite park.

Level

Supplies

- worsted-weight yarn (shown in various colors Bernat Sheep[ish] by Vickie Howell, and Bernat Sheep[ish] Stripes by Vickie Howell)
- yarn needle

Finished Size

Approximately 36" (91.5 cm), or desired length

Make It!

STEP 1. Holding two strands of yarn together as if they were one, yarn-wrap around four fingers—4 stitches.

STEP 2. Finger knit until the piece measures as long as desired, switching colors every 12" (30.5 cm) or so. The longer the strand (and the skinnier the branch you're wrapping it around), the more tree coverage!

STEP 3. Fasten off, leaving long tails for tying or sewing.

Finish It!

Wrap the piece(s) around the tree branches or the trunk. Use the long tails to tie or sew the tree cozy in place.

Hey, Art Teachers and Camp Leaders!

Yarn graffiti makes for a great group project. Have each kid make shorter pieces (in any color and texture). Then sew or tie the pieces together to create a larger cozy for a tree trunk at your school or local park.

Templates

Copy at 100%.

panda pillow

Finish It!

STEP 1. Scan and print templates for face and ears. Using templates as a guide, cut out felt pieces.

STEP 2. Pinch the ears to create a pleated effect, pin in place, and hand sew using a needle and thread.

STEP 3. Glue three layers of eyes, nose, and mouth pieces into place and let dry. If desired, reinforce the largest layer of eyes by sewing to the pillow cover around felt edges.

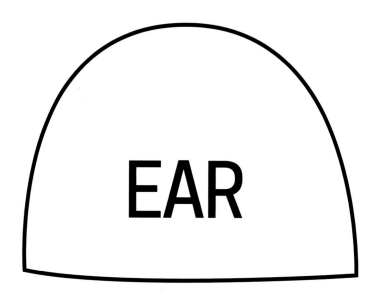

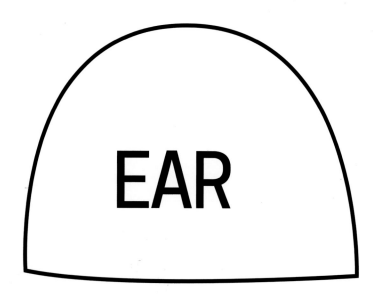

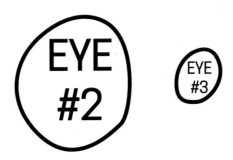

EYE
#1

EYE
#2

EYE
#3

MOUTH

NOSE

Suppliers

Yarnspirations
Patons, Bernat, Caron, Lily Sugar 'n Cream
www.yarnspirations.com

Cosmo Cricket
headband buttons
www.cosmocricket.com

Midori Ribbon
wrapping paper
www.midoriribbon.com

Tulip Dye
www.ilovetocreate.com

Acknowledgments

Thanks to the Primary Bluebirds at Khabele School for letting us invade their learning space to photograph in their classroom.

A huge shout out to TOMS, Austin, for letting us conduct a full day of photo shoots at their gorgeous space on South Congress. The staff couldn't have been more gracious, helpful, and generous with their time and space. Thank you!

To my friend and photographer, Cory Ryan: I had so much fun reuniting after a nine-year gap between gigs together. Working with another creative person who works hard and quickly was an absolute dream!

Thanks to our gorgeous models (and their parents) for their patience, smiles, and kind hearts: Manning Adkins, Sarah Bagh, Clover Campbell, Sofia Green, Tristan Howell, Mackenzie Kirsch, Daisy Sharp, Ruby Ku, Mina Tompkins, Robby Absalom, and Daniel Lindsay.

Sending much appreciation to Mary Ann Hall for coming to me with this sweet project and brainstorming every piece of the crafty puzzle with me, Betsy Gammons for wrangling all project details, Regina Grenier and Debbie Berne for making the book look purty, Rita Greenfeder for her tech editing magic, Kari Cornell for dotting the I's, crossing the T's, and managing my grammatically unfortunate love of commas, and Stefanie Girard, my old friend from *Knitty Gritty* days, for getting the word out to the kids that finger knitting is fun!

Last, but not least, I owe a bucketful of gratitude to my extraordinarily supportive husband, Dave Campbell, and to the children who inspire me every day: Tanner, Tristan, and Clover. I love you all to the moon and back, times infinity!

About the Author

Vickie Howell is a mother, designer, author, spokesperson, television host, and DIY lifestyles expert with a focus on the needle arts and creative parenting.

Vickie is most well-known as the host and creative consultant of DIY Network and HGTV's show, *Knitty Gritty*, her best-selling craft books, and her accessible, inclusive approach to nurturing the creative community via print, video, and social media. She's continued to rally the crafty troops through her work as the international spokesperson and creativity guide for the newly rebranded *Yarnspirations* (home of yarn giants, Patons, Bernat, Caron and Lily Sugar n' Cream), and is once again, knitting with viewers nationwide as the host of PBS' *Knitting Daily TV with Vickie Howell*.

Vickie is a board member of the Epilepsy Foundation of Central & South Texas and founder of *Purple Stitch Project* to benefit children with seizure disorders.

For more information on Vickie and her projects, go to www.vickiehowell.com. Follow her on social media @VickieHowell.

More Fun for Kids from Quarry Books!
Also available where ebooks are sold.

Kitchen Science Lab
ISBN: 978-1-59253-925-3

Art Lab for Kids
ISBN: 978-1-59253-765-5

3-D Art Lab for Kids
ISBN: 978-1-59253-815-7

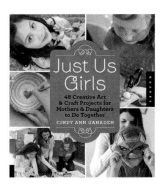

Just Us Girls
ISBN: 978-1-59253-890-4

The Paper Hat Book
ISBN: 978-1-59253-940-6

Knot Thread Stitch
ISBN: 978-1-59253-772-3

Print and Stamp Lab
ISBN: 978-1-59253-598-9

Noodle Kids
ISBN: 978-1-59253-963-5

Baking With Kids
ISBN: 978-1-59253-317-7